CW01642335

BOOK OF JOURNEYS

CHRISTOPHER A WRIGHT

Cover illustration by Sienna Wright - Instagram @siennachops

978-1-7394781-9-3

Originmarks.info : All text human generated, images human & machine generated. Cover image all human.

To Lilia & Sienna

who always leave the world considerably messier,

but ***way happier*** *than they found it.*

May your own adventures belong to you.

FOREWORD

WORDS AS SHAPER OF THE I-AS-WE: A REQUISITE PLANETARY SALVE

Frederick Luis Aldama

Frederick Luis Aldama, award-winning author of over 50 fiction, comics, and scholarly books as well as the Jacob & Frances Sanger Mossiker Chair in the Humanities at UT Austin. A Director on the board of The Academy of American Poets.

Walt Whitman opens his monumental poem “Song of Myself” thus: “I celebrate myself, and sing myself, / And what I assume you shall assume, / For every atom belonging to me as good belongs to you.” And with this and the lines that follow, Walt forever etches in our souls the singular self as *always already* a multitude of selves. “Myself” is only ever the interconnected self with all humans, organisms—planetary life.

Book of Journeys carries Walt’s deep understanding of our I-as-We interconnectedness into our contemporaneous world and its planetary denizens increasingly strangled, singed, and scorched by predatory governments, corporations, and rule of land warlordism. Predatory border patrollers, police, and human traffickers rape and murder without impunity. With the social tissue ripping apart, our capacity to realise our full potentialities in our togetherness is gasping for air. Extreme forms of exploitation, famine, and war force the displacement of millions of people from all corners of the globe: Iran, Ethiopia, Bangledesh, Nigeria, Dominican Republic, South Asia, El Salvador, Argentina, Chile, Nigeria, Ethiopia, Brazil, Taiwan, Malaysia, Vietnam, the Philippines, Mexico, Honduras, Nicaragua, Cuba, and Ukraine, among many other countries. Most of the planet's denizens carry scars of trauma and loss. Fear, suffering, and death blanket the Alpha to Omega of life.

Book of Journeys is about this—and more. It is the journey of the "I" in its reconnection with the "We"—the self with the multitudes. It's also an invitation for us to take pause and listen, taste, smell, touch, and see the world as it is, and as it may become. Its words in the form of poetry and prose, spin translucent yet resilient webs that transform the singular experience into the puissant collective.

As the poet voice makes clear, they are not of the displaced and cast out. They are not of the war-brandished and homeless. But those voices of the Ukrainians refugees are. Woven into the deep fabric of *Book of Journeys* are the voices of Alexandra Ievleva, Tereshenko Svitlana, Tatiana Odessa, Svetlana Groom, and Gubanova Julia. Their prose asks us to take pause and reflect on those humdrum rhythms of life that make a place, *home*—and how these can be violently taken from us at any given moment once again. Their stories tell of firsthand experiences with war—the destruction of homes, schools—life—by thundering tanks, exploding bombs, and puncturing bullets; the extreme suffering of the most vulnerable with their children and elders starving and shaking in underground shelters filled with the stench of death. Their stories remind of the violence that leads to death or displacement, coffins or suitcases, mass graves and mass border crossings.

Book of Journeys and the voices therein *are* more. In the face of war and tyranny, it's an invitation for us all to regroup as a compassionate collectivity. It's an invitation today to embark on a journey towards a tomorrow where we will create the material conditions for all planetary denizens to act as I-as-We agents of progressive, productive, and creative change. It's a celebration of the power of words to slow time and clear space for us to open to feel, care, and heal. Finally, it's a reminder that stories matter. They are our social glue. They are our collective unguent. They are our shared dreams of future journeys that lead the I-as-We—*home*.

INTRODUCTION

"Don't compare your life to others'. You have no idea what their journey is all about."

— **Regina Brett**

Regina is right.

In 2019 I met my friend Chris Lomas, erstwhile printer salesman, via a random connection on LinkedIn. His journey fascinated me. His wife, Zoe, had insisted they move to Moldova to help in the fight against human trafficking. And where others might have pointed out the impracticalities and dangers, he agreed.

Chris looks like me. White, middle class-ish, middle aged-ish. Non compliant-ish. All round -ish. And you may have noticed we're both Chris-ish. And yet here this other Chris was, in one of the poorest nations in the world, attempting change against a multi billion dollar industry organised by crime.

Reborn action man and activist.

A curious blend of envy, privilege-guilt and vicarious adventure drove me to follow their journey more closely. To boot, I was struck by the Lomas' ability to effect direct, powerful intervention with very little resource.

Every pound they got their hands on seemed to feed someone, fix something, *do* something.

And then Russia invaded Ukraine and we all watched as refugees flooded to the border, carrying lives in plastic bags and old wheelies.

What we didn't see on our live streams were the traffickers lying in wait, presenting as priests, kindly townsfolk, officials - ready to cash in and welcome the bumper payday of vulnerable men, women and children.

Something inside me changed as I struggled to take all of this in through Chris' visceral updates on social media.

Before then, I'd been the same as many of us. The refugee problem was desperate, but not my problem. Tragedies in boats and camps and politicised statistics. Someone else would fix it with my taxes, surely. People trafficking and modern slavery were in the same mental folder, with slightly less column inches. Someone else's tragic problem.

~

I decided to write this collection on a whim. The topic - journeys - set as a challenge by a friend.

I found it cathartic travelling memories of my own experiences through Europe, Asia, the USA and my own mind. To pick out pieces of the commute, the trains, planes and motorway service stations we frequent.

All whimsical observation and complaint, our British bread and butter, garnished with a smidgen of introspection and self realisation.

It wasn't until *Home* emerged from my pen that epiphany struck.

Home concerns two old English women discussing a refugee lady on the pavement below, asking people for help. "Oooh poor woman, how terrible, but she shouldn't have come here there's nothing for her". Somehow they managed to sound empathetic *and* utterly disdainful, all the while clutching their treasures from Marks & Sparks a little closer to their chests as if under threat.

I realised the refugee's journey was so *different* to mine. Here I was writing merrily about journeys through my own particular lens. Missed trains. Overpriced coffee. A boat trip. Things we can all identify with in our relatively comfortable existence.

But the stark contrast between my experience of Journey and "theirs" began to eat at me. Perhaps in contrasting the two, a little empathy could be forged. Perhaps some of the division and distance that separates "us" and "them" could be eaten away.

Why? Because once upon a time, the refugees and trafficking victims *were us*. The same as you and I. They were office workers, entrepreneurs, kids, dreamers, housewives, husbands, sons, daughters, uncles and aunts, shopkeepers, cleaners, clerics and clerical workers. They were the people who made up a community, proud of their country and living normal lives.

Look at the person across from you and imagine they were the one being pulled from the boat to a Royal Navy ship, given tea and a blanket before being sent for "processing".

The refugee stories you'll find throughout are direct translations of pieces sent to me from the people living that experience. Aside from small corrections and very minor edits, they are unchanged and raw. Some are humdrum, some are horrific and some show the amazing capacity of humans for compassion.

This is not a book crying for donations or help. There are many problems in the world, including our own very real issues. Mostly, it's a little collection of poems to dip into as an occasional companion. I've snuck in my Ukrainian friends' voices to show our contrasting worlds and hope you'll read their stories alongside mine.

It would be nice if the world inched towards being a better place for you having done so.

JOURNEYS

"All this hurrying from place to place won't bring you any relief, for you're travelling in the company of your own emotions, followed by your troubles all the way."

— Seneca, Letters from a Stoic

WIND

For those few seconds
Where the jets accelerate to take off speed.
I am adventurer. Spaceman. Racer. King.
Free from earth. Free from mind. I am wind.

GLÜCKLICH

When the East German Police left our carriage
And the glückliches schoolgirl pulled the dope from her blouse
I finally saw the real world, wild
In the realms beyond my house

MUSKY

Where is my damn rocket-ship!
I am done with cars.
Two dimensions? Not enough.
I want Mars.

VICTORIA

Victoria Coach Station at midnight
holds no adventurous anticipation
only weary dread ahead
of six hours squished shoulder to shoulder
and elbows silently fighting for arms.
No sleep, no dreams, no qualms.

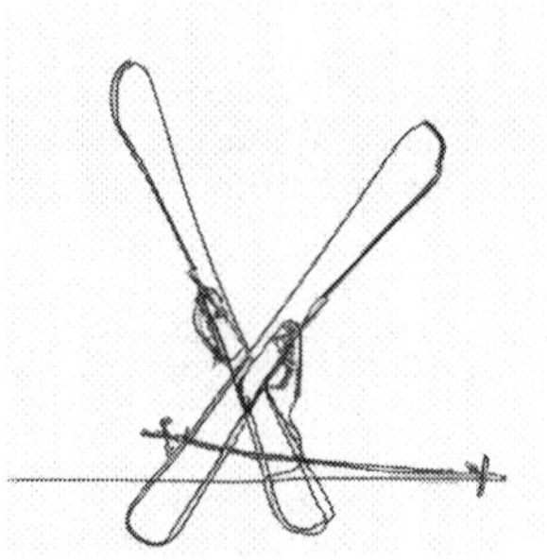

THE BEGINNING

...to relax in the thermal springs in Kosyno, and to put our son on skis for the first time.

Good evening, here is my personal story "The Beginning of the War".

We lived a quiet, measured life... We had dreams, desires, goals and plans... All different... Find a new job, join a gym, have a wedding, renovate our flat, finish our driving course...

On the 24th of February at 3 am we left Odessa in the direction of the Carpathians for a pre-planned holiday.

We wanted to go skiing, to enjoy the beauty of snow-covered mountains, to savour delicious Transcarpathian cuisine, to relax in the thermal springs in Kosyno, and to put our son on skis for the first time.

Two hours after we left (at 5 in the morning) we got a phone call from my mum who said there were 3 huge bombs near Odessa airport. We immediately googled on the phone and found out that we were being attacked by Russia.

— **Alexandra Ievleva**

FUJI

Konohanasakuya-hime lives on Fuji San
So bring your trash home
You know you can.

DREAMERS

After I wake up from dreams,
do the dream friends I had
see me leave?
Are they aware that their tormentor and tormentee –
just disappeared?

Did I leave a wispish thread of me?

TEA

I found myself that day somehow enveloped in a tea ceremony, ad hoc staged for my benefit in the back office of a Taiwan bottle factory.
My host's wife, elegant and mysterious and old to my young eyes was, I understood, a big thing in tea ceremony world.

Tall cup.
Feel.
Short cup.
Smell.
Breathe.
Absorb.
Behold. The Universe!

The Universe and all her secrets are there for you in this formality, foreigner.

老外

Yet I saw nothing but tea.

INSOMNIA

1am, 2am, 3am
Why is the dawn escape
So far away?

SERVICES

Every 3am guest at a service station
Has a curious story behind them —
There are no normals then.
You linger amongst the lost, the loopy, the lovers
The junk food addicts and late returning revellers
The early morning adventurers obsessed with system
The hustlers and the hustled
The band and the band-aids
The salesman avoiding the game.
No-one has a place to go but here
A place to hide from the places they fear

HOME

I overhear two old women on a south London bus-top
"So many of them. I don't know why they come"
There's a nod to compassion in her voice
as she privately berates the life-beaten woman
holding out her hand for hope of help at the bus-stop below
"There's nothing for them here, we haven't got enough for our own!"
And I wonder what fires the below-lady escaped
What gunpoints she faced
What terrors she tricked in her race to freedom
And where is her final stop for home?

THE CATS

There was no time to stop by my house to pack some things, so I left as I was: a bag of pants and the clothes I was wearing, the cats and their food.

The shops were almost empty. By some miracle, someone was bringing in bread. As long as we had flour and light, Vera baked by herself. Cooking calmed her down - it was something she could control. I could only try to calm the cats and clean their litter box on time - I could control that, it calmed me down.

Every day there was a debate: Vera's husband insisted that we had to leave, Vera insisted that it was dangerous to leave, let's wait a little longer, maybe they would make a green corridor. Tomorrow it would become clear that we should have left yesterday because things were getting worse and worse.

One evening, during the curfew, it was decided I go at my own risk tomorrow, as soon as the curfew was over, in the morning. I could be taken, but without cats - there wasn't much room.

The family had two cars, my husband's and Alexei's, and the plan was to drive both, taking as many people as possible. But Alexei could not find gasoline instead of the one he spent on the rescue, so there was only one car and a lot of things.

I cried twice since February 24: when I found out how that pregnant girl had got to Vera, and when I was put before the choice of leaving on my own or staying with the cats. I couldn't leave them.

Luckily for me, the next morning my husband (it was his condition) changed his mind.

There was no time to stop by my house to pack some things, so I left as I was: a bag of pants and the clothes I was wearing, the cats and their food.

– Tereshenko Svitlana

BITTER

Surely by now I should understand
The coffee I buy from this stand
Will not enhance my synaptic efficiency
Will not add three pounds fifty to my life
It will likely end up lukewarm
And tossed to the side.
But I *do* understand this truth -
This coffee was an easy and warm excuse
To laugh with the Philippina coffee girl
And for a fleeting moment, escape from my world

RIVERFOLK

Morning clinks and steams and waves from the moored
Before 10 am they're friendly enough, I've heard

START

It's 7 am and I head for the bar
Full English breakfast, hash browns and a beer
What mysterious and exotic land is this here,
This, Heathrow

DISTURBANCE

The solo runner
picked her way
down the path
on the opposite
side of the cove,
startling the beach gulls.
Flash-anger!
My crafted calm dismantled
Not anger with her.
Anger because
she would be the
first of many
thoughts that day.

ELECTRIC

"Make sure it's fully charged tonight"
Of course, I didn't
I failed in my charge of charging and am duly charged
with travel negligence and trip ruin.
But perhaps it was a subconscious plan?
One that ran to extract that secret win
of a sneaky Greggs that shouldn't have been?

THE BREAKDOWN

And at that moment he said: "Mom, I don't want to die!!!"

We didn't know what the right thing to do at this particular moment was - to keep going to the Carpathians or to go back to Odessa. Because the thought of war was just not in our heads, and our brain, heart and soul simply refused to believe it!!!! This cannot be!!!

Perhaps at that moment a sign from on high was needed to help us make the right decision? And there it was - a sign.

Our car gave us an error on the screen and soon stalled on Kiev highway, near Umaniya, not far from an ammunition depot that was just being shelled by planes and ammunition started exploding so violently that our stalled car was shuddering and wobbling!

My legs had never been so shaky in my life, they literally began to bounce with fear, but I tried to control myself and reassure my son.

And at that moment he said: "Mom, I don't want to die!!!" It was very scary!

We all had different dreams, wishes, goals and plans...

Now we have ONE dream, ONE wish, ONE goal, ONE plan - to WIN! To drive the vile, vile and pathetic terrorist occupiers from our homeland! Show the world that we are a strong independent state!!!

We will not let anyone dictate our terms to us!!! We won't let anyone take away our dreams, devalue our desires, cross out our goals, break our plans!

Glory to Ukraine!!!

Glory to the heroes!!!

The victory is ours!!!

Death to the enemy!!!

— **Alexandra Ievleva**

LAYBY

A chicken sandwich appears from the front seat
I'm told it's special, Marks and Sparks.
I think it tastes of petrol but I persevere.
The car occasionally wobbles from passing trucks.
Eat the sandwich. Get the snacks.
I don't know how many hours in we are.
How many left. How far.
Walkman batteries running low.
Eat the sandwich. Then we can go.

TRAINED

"We hope you have a pleasant onward journey"
Have you ever heard such cynical wording?
Before the pirate leaves the plank at dawn
"We hope the water's nice and warm!"

My pleasant onward journey, dear, *dear* disembodied train voice
 person,
is about to begin with a gaggle of morons.
A ticket machine that will refuse my ticket.
An officious inspector who's far from efficient.
The screaming Jubilee to deafen me
all before my glorious city
will welcome me gladly
with open arms.
Her charms.
Free.

BORACAY

Right after takeoff
the pilot grinned, welcoming us.
Beer in hand

KOWLOON

I didn't know where I was
I didn't know who I was
I just walked.
Perhaps the length of Kowloon
No reason but to see
And smell
And listen
Perhaps the length of China
I had no idea
But *what* I saw!
What I smelled!
What I heard!
Perhaps I never left Star Harbour
It didn't matter
I was there. I was I.
Walking.

GAP

From where you are
To where you want -
That's the Gap.
Should the Gap get smaller,
Or bigger?
Is bigger wiser, and smaller older?
Or smaller wiser and bigger older?
Is one naive and the other bolder?
Do you believe what gurus told you?

UNITED

Why do travelling strangers,
AKA — enemies
Crammed and tired and seething hatred
Suddenly unite as one,
As friends and saviours
Empaths and entertainers
Joining forces as family
Just because the train unfathomably
Refuses to travel dutifully?
I like to think it's because humanity
Is more human than we think it be.

LIVINGSTONES

The discovery of a previously undiscovered neighbourhood
Is living proof of the existence of a universal Good
Alive in the noise and grime of this London hum
As any far away jungles of the Amazon

THE TULIPS

We passed some small town: it was quiet, the sun was shining, and the men were buying tulips. As if nothing was going on fifty kilometers away. Nothing. Vera and I were both square-eyed: was it a dream?

It was the first time in more than two weeks that I'd seen the city as we drove out. Potholes in the asphalt, urchins in the roads, blocks across the road, broken houses, broken windows, signs of fires, tree trunks chopped to splinters. We queued for more than three hours in the queue for the bridge to the constant cannonade of artillery. We stood and prayed. It was very scary, though we understood that our people were shooting, we went there, where they were shooting at our people. A Russian tank burnt, a burnt-out car, houses shot and burnt out, a village crumbled beyond recognition and a turn to the hare tracks to bypass Yagodnoye.

It was the eighth of March.

We passed some small town: it was quiet, the sun was shining, and the men were buying tulips. As if nothing was going on fifty kilometres away. Nothing. Vera and I were both square-eyed: was it a dream?

Or was what we had experienced a dream? Our boys at the checkpoints were congratulating us, and handing back our passports, and we were both roaring with joy.

At one of the checkpoints, they would not let us go forward: there were Russian tanks, and there would be fighting. They offered to wait, saying it was not the first time, ours usually beat them back. The battle did not take place that day, and we were faced with the question of spending the night. One of the variants - to return home and try again tomorrow - threw Vera and me into a state of terror: we began to breathe only when we understood: we left.

By some miracle, we met people who gave us keys to the house, which was only used in summer and now was vacant. The house faced the highway, and I could hear the heavy cars all night. I couldn't see because the windows were tightly shut: a strict light disguise. It was freezing: an uninhabited house in winter. I could not sleep - all night long I had to keep the cats quiet in their carriers: I had to let those who could sleep.

– **Tereshenko Svitlana**

NYC

90's New York City:
"Taxi driver! Take me somewhere
I need music!"

"This is New York, boy!
I could drop you anywhere.
People die here!"

Luckily, no death.
Only the brightest *son et lumière*
Of feathers and sequins and acrylic hair.

HORIZON

To see the horizon at all four points
Is to see why we need each other

PACKED

The boy
With dog
And bear
Was moved

Again.

New friends
No friends
Just dog
And bear

STOPS

No matter how many changes
No matter how many stops
Barrier hops
Underground waits
Overground wails
Stairwells
Escalators
Elevators
Uphills,
Rickety spills –

To you, it's worth it

FLOW

The moment when
the harbour was behind me,
so was life

THE POOL

...burned the columns of vehicles on the outskirts, blew up two bridges over the rivers to prevent the enemy from crossing quickly...

On March 1, they were attacking Voznesensk. My two children and my parents and I were forced to stay in the basement of a five-story building, it was scary, cold and dark, the lights were turned off, we found flashlights with batteries and watched the news with neighbours, the alarms were not removed.

We had to spend the night on pallets in the basement, local cats saved us from the cold, they knelt down at night and warmed us with their warmth.

Our "cats" of the Armed Forces of Ukraine and the local Territorial defence troops repelled the attack on the city, burned the columns of vehicles on the outskirts, blew up two bridges over the rivers to prevent the enemy from crossing quickly, but the Rashists were shooting in the city centre, first of all at the communications, hit the telegraph tower, then hit the pool in the middle of residential buildings.

The shooting was heard in the basement, it was very scary because of the unknown future. We just wrote short messages to relatives and friends - "we are alive".

— **Orel Natalia**

TAXI

How many times
should English thank the taxi
before we leave?

BREAK

To peer over Cornish cliffs to the seas
Is to peer into mortality
As the rocks and waves whisper to me
I'm saved by sweet Roskilly

SE19

The cafes of south London
Cobbled up lovingly by locals
Feed the soul far more richly
than the boulevards of St James

The cafes of south London
Welcome you as friends
Embrace you with knick-knacks
Stories, personal blends.

The cafes of south London
Do not want to take, like the boulevards do
They simply exist
To be a part of you

A50

On winter nights
cars running on willpower alone
should avoid running

AMSTERDAM

I lost myself
In Disneyland for the lost
Until I reached the bar
And found the curious salvation
Of the Devil and a Dutch

GPS

“Make sure to
turn left at the lights!”
Good old days.

THE TEA

All the way, I had a feeling of absolute defencelessness, as if a bug was crawling on the glass and there was nowhere to hide.

At precisely 6 in the morning, once the curfew was over, we hit the road again. It turned out that the cars that were standing with us at the checkpoint had taken a diversion to Kyiv - the locals had made a diversion. The road was not cleared. That fight took place, we saw it later on the news.

We took a diversion too. At each checkpoint they warned us not to go in one direction: the Russians were seen there.

All the way, I had a feeling of absolute defencelessness, as if a bug was crawling on the glass and there was nowhere to hide.

I like expensive loose-leaf tea without sugar, sachets are the evil one, I was sure.

But you should have known how delicious, sweet Tess tea was in a roadside cafe somewhere in the Zhytomyr region, where we made our first stop on our own - to drink hot tea. The tea was magical.

All in all, the journey to Chisinau from Chernihiv this time took 68 hours instead of the usual 10-11.

– Tereshenko Svitlana

SEATED

There are only two acceptable seats on the bus to Brixton
The one at the top at the front and the one next to you

HINCKLEY

I was once asked
why I felt the need
to travel beyond
the village walls
if everything was here.

I answered:

Because if that's what you believe, then *I* cannot be here.

NEDERLAND

Population today 1532.
Say hello to Bredo, Mr.
Welcome to Nederland.

RIVERBOAT

Buy your riverboat
Go left
Go right
Drink gin
Fight
Fuss
Repeat
Sell your riverboat
Be free

GLASS

What world is behind that slab of glass you hold to your nose
more fascinating than your fellow travellers,
with instant stories written on faces, bags and clothes

REDEYE

Step from a redeye into a cold dawn terminal of a new city.
Reborn. Suckling coffee instead of milk. Collared up anonymity.
Homeless packing up makeshift beds. Cigarettes.
Messages checked.
Non-plussed workers numbe(re)d by grind
Moving in unison. Following signs.
Clockwork clock workers. All in flow.
Their system, I can't follow.

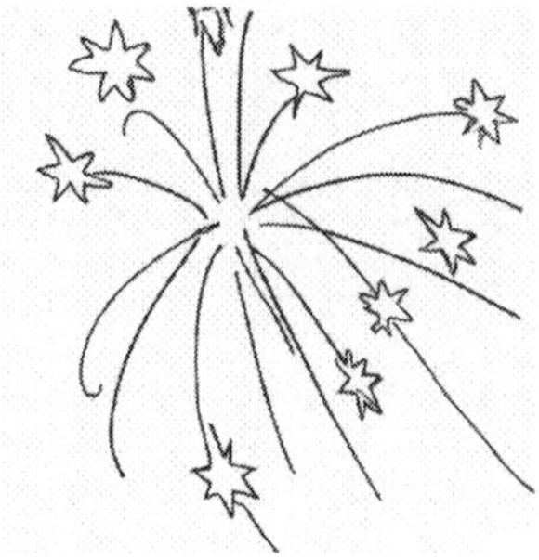

THE FIREWORKS

We sat in the flat all day, nervously smoking, drinking coffee, and not eating anything.

It was an ordinary day, 23 February 2022. My husband and children and I had had fun and went to bed happily.

I heard an explosion in the early hours of 24 February 2022. To my sleepy senses it was fire-works. And I fell asleep again. I woke up to a call from my sister at 6am, my sister in tears saying to me, "War!!!" I told her: "it can't be".... I put the phone down and started to go on social media and read the horror and realised it was not fireworks, but explosions.

Crying, don't know what to do, daughter 12 years asleep, son 1 year 3 months, also asleep. I woke up my husband and said: "Get up, the war has started!" My husband and I are nervously walking around the flat not knowing what to do.

We sat in the flat all day, nervously smoking, drinking coffee, and not eating anything. Panic, psychosis, tears, fear for the children. We packed a bag just in case. I looked out of the window all day and watched people leave in a hurry. I said to my husband: "We should also leave, we live in a multi-storey building, what if there is a rocket landing?"

We decided to go to my parents' house the next day. We went to bed with our clothes on, but we didn't get much sleep, the anxiety was terrible. On 25

February 2022 we woke up and started to think where else we could go... we didn't want to go anywhere; our brain wasn't accepting it... the world was exploding inside us.

— **Gubanova Julia**

MAIDENHEAD

Sitting down and apologising, Englishly, to the lady opposite
whose bags and treasures had been spread defensively across the table
she curls and cocoons into her earpods, feigning sleep
as I carefully arrange my own paraphernalia
taking care not to pass the imaginary halfway mark of the train table
as home-bounders file past in search of seats
and the stranger and I combine our mental forcefields to repel the
    invaders,
the exhausted, drunk and fast-food-loaded legionnaires of the 23:20
when from my hiding place I feel a bump
as an ogre lands beside, spilling shopping bags and elbows and knees
and without looking I pull my coffee cup a little closer along with
    my Self
and begin the prayer for Maidenhead to arrive.

SEVEN

Woke up on day seven
To push the haziness
Just far enough
For expert laziness
Until bed again

LAUNDRY

Lost off a trail in Kamakura
Rain blinding and incessant
A kindly alien lady signalled to follow

The kindly alien smiled the way
Hand signals and nods and kindly alien eyes
We arrived at the alien's favourite place and
Kindly alien signalled she wanted money

Bah!

So
That's
The
Deal!

Then —

She carefully took the tiny coins I kindly offered
And kindly, carefully washed them with her alien hands

In the Zeniarai Benten spring

LASER-CAKE

Nation states
Should race
To eat cake
In space
Instead of
Nasty laser bases
Ending human races
Because
With cakes
In faces
Who could misplace

Humanity.

ARRIVAL

I awoke on the floor of the Yugoslavian's apartment somewhere in
Frankfurt.
Yesterday I was a boy. Politely raised. Eager to please. Airs and grace.

But now I'd tasted slivovitz.

HOLE

The inescapable hole
Left by the thing that escaped
Made this new whole
Uncomfortably shaped

MEET

“STOP!” said the new client boss.
I was in an APM (Always-Pointless-Meeting),
And I’d been caught autonomic spieling.
“Just stop.”
She put down her coke slowly, for emphasis.
“You’re so bored with this!”
She was right.
Time for a new adventure.
I’d sleep well that night.

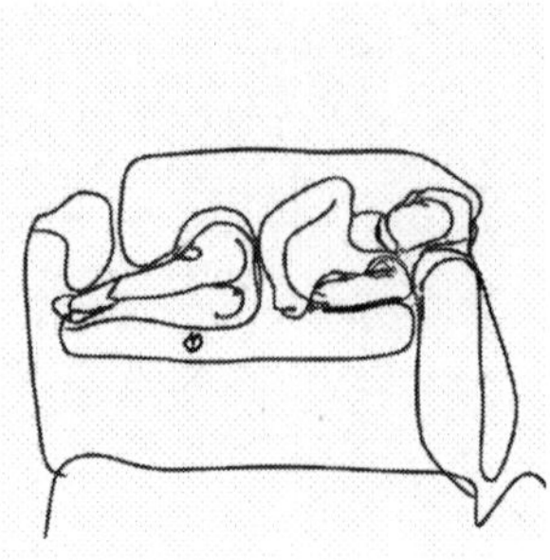

THE SUITCASE

My 14-year- old daughter came into the room and said: "Why are you lying down? Get up. Let's pack a suitcase"

On 24 February, I went out into the street and saw huge queues of cars. People were rushing to leave the city. I didn't immediately realise that a lot of things were about to change. So, like every day, I drove to work. In the empty office there was only security and an accountant. I tried to do my job, but I could not think straight. Towards lunchtime there was a loud bang. My children called me. They were frightened, because the explosion shook our multi-storey house, and they were home alone.

When I got home, I started looking for somewhere to take the children. For all the suggested destinations, transport had either been cancelled or all the tickets were sold out. I was desperate because I was bringing them up on my own and I had no one to consult. After exploring what I thought were all the options, horrified and shocked, I was lying on the sofa in tears and didn't know what to do.

I don't know how long my state of shock would have lasted had it not been for the children. My 14-year-old daughter came into the room and said: "Why are you lying down? Get up. Let's pack a suitcase".

– **Tatiana Odessa**

SCONE

As I travel West
I begin to worry
What's best?
Jam then cream, or cream then jam?
Does it even matter in this endless traffic jam?
And where does the law change exactly?
After the county line, now behind me?
Or is there a no man's land of jammy cream?
Where I can mix it up, like in a dream?
But for now, the Lizard is hours away.
So I guess stick with stuff from Gregg's today.

LEFT

Some days I panic:

Are there enough trips left in me
To see all the world I want to see?
To meet the people I need to meet
To live the dreams I've always dreamed?

And then –
I breathe.

DRUM

Like smokers bound by common cause
Shunned to doorways in rain and wind
So are electric car drivers seeking juice
“Got far to go?”
“How many miles you gettin’?”
I mourn the old me that dies a little

CARRY

Exasperation is unmatched when snatched from above us our locker
space is erased without trace and we are forced to chase the down-
plane race to find a place to stash our case.

SIDE-EYE

I catch the guy's screen next to me
We scroll his roll
A private guided tour of his life
I imagine he watches Love Island
And quickly leave

TRANSIENT

It was Amsterdam
A hotel bar, at the bar
She was a Finn, studying
He was a New York, Puerto Rican, pilot
I sat between them, drinking
I hope they lived happily ever after

THE HYSTERIA!

I cried and was worried about my husband and parents, that they could not come with us.

Hysteria!

We came with my husband and children to my parents' house. We stayed with them until 01 March 22 and in the evening, we decided that the children, my sister and I should go to Moldova. We do not have anyone we know in Moldova. My sister and I sent a message to a telegram group (Help for Ukrainians in Moldova) and thank God people responded. We were told that we could come to them in Chisinau and live with them for free.

02 March 22. In the morning we quickly got ready, from nerves I could not eat at all. I cried and was worried about my husband and parents, that they could not come with us. They wouldn't let the men out, and it was like the ground was slipping from under my feet. My husband came to pick us up and said he would take us to the Moldovan border. Our husbands came with us to say goodbye and see us off. When we arrived at the border, we saw a huge convoy of cars, so we decided to walk 3 km to the border. It would have been quicker that way.

I was carrying a pram with my son sleeping in it, my daughter was carrying several packs of nappies and my husband was carrying 2 suitcases with my belongings. The goodbye was very hard, my tears made me feel nauseous and dizzy... a lump in the throat. We crossed the border and my sister, my children and I just stood in the rain and didn't know what to do. I was crying, the children were crying, my sister was running around looking for volunteers to take us to Chisinau. There were many volunteers, but someone wanted $500 to take us, someone was already busy and could not take us. Suddenly, a guy named Gheorghe comes up and asks: “Where should we go? I’m paying”, and I say: “to Chisinau, but we don’t have any money”. Gheorghe said, “What money? Let’s go.

Do you know the address where they’re waiting for you”? I said yes. So, we loaded our things into his car, and we drove off. On the way, Gheorghe bought us some food, coffee, and tea. He was very kind and a nice person who met us on the way, thanking us very much. Gheorghe took us to where people were waiting for us in Chisinau. We were met by a young couple. Anna and Marius, they took us in. We stayed with them for a month. After that, the guys had to go to another country for their studies and we were asked to find another place to live. We found an announcement in a telegram group that we could live in a large house outside Chisinau. Refugees from Ukraine also live in that house. We called and were told that we were homeless, that we were from Odessa.

— **Gubanova Julia**

BOATMAN

"I'm sorry I don't have enough cash on me right now to pay for the boat
I just booked tomorrow I still owe you what, twenty, but I already
paid the eighty should I run back to my room now and get it for you
how long will you be here I mean will you be open for another hour
or maybe I can find you in a bar somewhere near here later and give
it to you then, shit I'm so sorry I thought I had the cash now but
forgot I bought lunch earlier and it was more than I expected and..."

The boatman laughed at me
"Relax! This is Koufonisia, not England"
I understood.

BIOLUMINESCENT

The boy handed me an old Evian bottle
The small plastic kind that crinkles when you squish it
It was wrapped with fishing line and a hook
Our tiny boat pushed off the beach
Moonlight
Noctiluca scintillans glowed blue green
And we silently pushed past their sleepy heads
One by one my new friends caught fish to my none
And I caught memories

RUSH

Why
Why do
Why do people
People with the most
The most complicated journeys imaginable
Journeys with the most complicated circuitous routes
Demand circuitous and unnecessary questioning of the seller
The seller who at best operates on half speed
Why do those people insist on buying tickets before me?

PICCADILLY

Taxi, London, Piccadilly.
Sir, I walked from Eritrea!
This is easy!

DEAL

I stared past the filth
At my eyes staring back
The journey here stank
This bathroom stank
This situation stank.
Get it together!
One *next* last chance
One *next* last fork to choose
One *next* last shot to escape this shit

THE CROISSANTS

For another month I was cold all the time. I couldn't keep warm even under two blankets. At night, when the children were asleep, I could allow myself to cry.

A day later we were in Moldova. We barely made it through customs. At that time, in the very first days of the war, minors were not allowed out without the permission of the other parent. And we did not have one.

On the other side of the border a volunteer met us and asked: "Can I help you?" And I burst into tears.

My children were happy for the free croissants - they had pockets full of them. We were taken to the nearest big town.

For another month I was cold all the time. I couldn't keep warm even under two blankets. At night, when the children were asleep, I could allow myself to cry. For the pain. Because my beloved country was being destroyed. My people - men and women - are being tortured, raped and murdered. For nothing. For the fact that we are Ukrainians. I wept in pain for my orphaned children, for the maimed and murdered.

These days the pain of every Ukrainian has become my pain. It remains so.

– **Tatiana Odessa**

WINCHESTER

The old lady of the Scriptorium,
Winchester Cathedral,
Is not one to be trifled with.
She spends her days amongst ancient texts
Willing tourists to ask
Something better
Than "What's next?"
Something more
Than "ooh, did they use candles then?"
A hundred years of human.
A thousand years of humans.
All wrapped up by her,
The old lady of the Scriptorium.
To fall prey to her –
Is to fall headfirst into magic

COIN

Father gives money
to the homeless he sees,
mayhap it’s me

23:35

The connecting train driver
believes waiting a moment
will destroy the timetable.

Masochist pain thriver

LAWN

The man who marched across the lawn
Not in a straight line
Not quietly like me
Was not sad to be leaving

He sang of triumph!
The man who marched across the lawn
Fine fettled and feisty
Open container rules be damned

Travellers eyed cautiously
As his lungs burst and eyes popped
The man who marched across the lawn
Perhaps he was a threat?

Travellers were wrong.
He was happy to be alive!
Happy to commune with Isembard!
The man who marched across the lawn

LIST

Passport
Charger
Cash
Cards
Mouthguard
Stash
Now —
Where to go?

OY

To sit and shuck
And slurp and chuck
Upon the Whitstable stones
Is to be at one
With the one
And never feel alone

THE ATM

Instead of a blooming, stylishly dressed woman, I had a grandmother standing in front of me with trembling hands.

In the past, not so long ago (but it seems like in another life), my father-in-law always said one toast: “May there be peace, health and a harvest”. But there is peace! And it seemed that it would always be there. It's true what we have, we don't keep, and when we lose, we cry...

For me the war started with a huge queue at a petrol station in the district centre, and then at an ATM, where a huge crowd had gathered.

When I asked my question: “What happened?” they looked at me like I was stupid and said that a war had broken out. I remember general panic and depression - all the usual life went down in an instant. And when it started to come...

More and more often, we realised that we had to save the dearest thing we had - our little grandson - and we decided to leave. And recently here, in Chisinau, there was a meeting that shook me to the core.

A woman passed in front of me, who seemed vaguely familiar to me, and I rushed to catch up with her. I overtook her and stood like a rock - it was my former colleague, who after retirement left for her daughter in Nikolaev. But my God! Instead of a blooming, stylishly dressed woman, I had a grandmother standing in front of me with trembling hands. We were both crying...

For 20 days she had been sitting in the basement of her apartment building, practically without food or water, unable even to wash properly. And now my only toast is, "Let there be peace!!!"

– **Eugenia Yermeni Mikolaev**

LAND

Narita is grey
A colour of nothing
Maybe beige?
Like a smoker's ceiling

Signs to obey
Cotton gloved poking
A stage
For adventuring

I Escaped!
Rice fields swaying
Tightly spaced
Tokyo calling

Pay day!
Takeshita Dori
A maze.
Amazing.

TOURRETTES

Is it wrong, when faced with yet another mediaeval French village,
All oohs and aahs and cobblestoned walkways,
Fortified walls, tall narrow streets and crumbly houses
Is it wrong to suggest we sit and drink wine and eat bread instead?

S(H)IT

"He'll just spend it on drugs or drink!"
You think?
Does it matter?
Sat here amongst the shit and bullshit of our bourgeoisie
I am fairly sure his day could use it more than me

MOVE

I think of places I haven't been
With sand and cigars and cars and scenes
From a movie that has yet to be
And I think so hard
A smile appears

STEPS

These steps we make —
These ten thousand tiny steps.
How many are left?

GLASTIC

One by one I survey the characters in this Centraal plastic cafe
Seated at the white plastic tables,
queuing at the glass and steel counter as
they peer at the pastries and breakfast sandwiches
before choosing an automated coffee to guzzle.
Already bamboozled by the day
each one hunches over their phone
sliding and poking for tiny dopamine hits
to go with their twin caffeine and sugar hits.
Each one is crushed to the shape of a C
by an invisible collapsing weighty ceiling.

Come on! The fucking departure board says Vienna, Paris, London,
  Berlin!
The very thing you swipe to see is just beyond these plastic seats!

OVERSHOT

I was barely awake.
Correction. I wasn't awake.
I see that now as clear as I see this station name.
Not my station.
Not my beautiful nearly-made-it, almost-in-bed station.
This station spells pain-in-the-assness.
How-do-I-get-homeness.
I'm done with adventuring.
Taxi. Credit card OK?

THE TALYANKA

Yes, you're front-line friends, yes, you're front-line brides

The lady of the ball, the queen of the ball. Like an ugly fairy-tale duckling, the beautiful swan.

When, in the morning, another artillery raid, and an explosion rips off your tent-coat, you get a sight like Ophelia, with the tender sound of a *talyanka.*

In the morning artillery raids again, the tent cloak will be torn off by the explosion... The sky will seem like a corkscrew to the howling and bursting of shells... I wish I could hide somewhere in a hollow, but I think you say to myself: "I must!".

Someone called out: "Sis! Help, help, my dear!"

And you drag him to the side to shield him from a bullet. Yes, you're front-line friends, yes, you're front-line brides.... But isn't there no place for girls to fall in love under the roar of guns?

May you all live to see victory, cherish your children and grandchildren. Under peaceful and tender skies all you need is your good hands! But death spared no one... War... It's all so hard... In countless mass graves lie the frontline nurses.

– **Eugenia Yermeni Mikolaev**

BERKELEY

The year we spent Christmas in San Francisco
Was the year I spent waiting for Christmas.

Because it wasn't *my* Christmas.
The icons were wrong. The symbols were wrong.
The bingo list of end of year bookmarks to mark off
were lost in the frame of someone else's day.

How did I miss that?
Their beautiful way?

NEON

To step into the warm electric moons of August Tokyo,
sharp eyed from the techno and four beat adrenaline flow —
is to feel neon-invincible against invisible night foes

WINDOW

How do we sleep standing?
Hypnagogic between stations
Chrysalises, stuck balancing
Between window and commuter's baggages
Anchored by monotonous wheel noise
Thrown by the off-beat screech of pissed party boys

Awoken when

"We'll soon be arriving in –"

TIP

The brown boy eagerly took my bag from me
somehow balancing it above the water
as he steered my clumsiness from the boat.
With a smile at shore he held out a hand
and I, newly arrived and English, panicked.
This strange money had no value and there were so many notes.
I'm English, he's ripping me off I'm sure!
It's his bloody job to meet me at the boat!
I hand over something that strikes me as small and fair.
Brown boy disappears to the next arrival and I to my next stage.
I still see the disappointed disgust in his eyes.
To me, that wasn't even a polystyrene coffee –
To him, it was a week's wages.
I still wonder about that Englishman I was

SUNSETS

Food and wine
Tuscan sunset. Friends. Laughter. Debate.
That was living.

TRIP

When you first land
When your toes touch sand
When you step back in time
When you've left behind
When you climb castle towers
When you sit for hours
When you taste their food
When you leave your hotel room
When you've truly arrived
When the trip is real —

How do you feel?

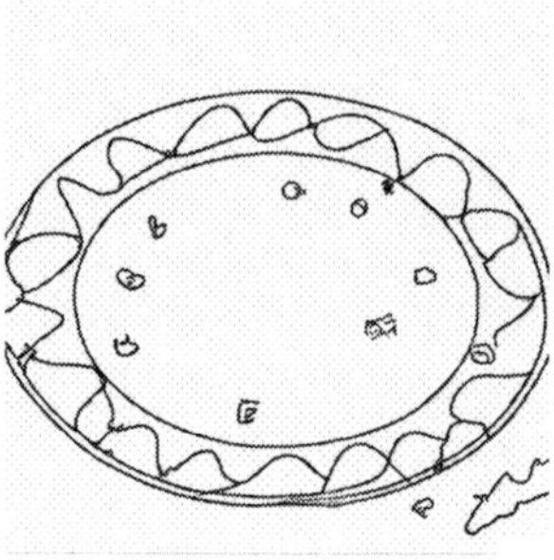

THE CAKE

No war film, no book about its horrors, no memoirs, no talent of narrator could make you feel fully what we were going through at that moment. Fear and rage.

Grandma's Napoleon cake is one of the tastiest things in my world. It takes all day to make, but it's well worth it.

On 22 February I saw ready-made cakes for it in the shop and decided to try it with the family cream recipe - it's a huge time saver.

The 23 February was a very active day: in the morning my sister called me and said that there would be a long-awaited delivery to Chisinau, but today I have to send the parcel to Odessa, where they will take it. So, since morning I gathered everything I wanted to give to my family: a series of Harry Potter books, clothes for the whole family, medicine, sweets, which I wanted to please my nephew.

By lunchtime the packages had been sent, and I was exhausted - I'd been working all night and hadn't slept since Tuesday, in fact, and there was still a lot to do. I thought: the rest is tomorrow, it's not going anywhere. So I went home to sleep.

After resting, I decided not to put it off and went where I was going: to pick up the cat food I had ordered and to take a cake to my friend and her family. I went to the drugstore and bought band-aids.

How happy I was the next day and the fact that my cats have food and that food (a hearty cake) I have and that there are patches - I had a wound that requires special treatment after a small operation. I already had plans for 24 February: I was going to start sewing a complicated order. Everything I needed was already packed and waiting on my desk.

I woke up very early, anticipating a day of concentrated work. I switched on my laptop, sat down to breakfast, checking my messages. And I heard an explosion. From that moment on, I lost track of time.

The days merged into one sleepless interval full of alternating daily shelling of the city and horrible, wild, unbelievable news and swearing at pro-Russian relatives.

Chernihiv region borders both Belarus and Russia. Near the Ukrainian border village of Senkivka there is a statue called “Three Sisters”, a monument to the friendship of the peoples of the three neighbouring countries. Festivals used to take place there. Not anymore.

From the border in a straight line to Chernigov it is 60-70 kilometres, on the highway - 80. It's nothing for tanks. They started shelling Chernigov at once, trying to occupy the city.

No war film, no book about its horrors, no memoirs, no talent of narrator could make you feel fully what we were going through at that moment. Fear and rage.

– **Tereshenko Svitlana**

DAUGHTERS

Sometimes I need the sea
Not to sail on, swim or fish
Just to see
2.174 miles,
blue to the horizon,
uninterrupted,
barrier free —
So I can see
what you mean to me

TUNNEL

Can you hear me now?
This route is dark
Fuck. Tunnel.
If you could hear me,
I'd tell you
these tunnel lights
fly past
like life
how these cables
rise and fall —
like life
If you could hear me
I'd tell you
all the things I have balled up insi...

hello?

I'll be there in about 15. Yeah, see you later.

LAMENTO

The end began when the flamenco began
in that musty church with sunbeams and dust
and I realised - there must be more to living than us

BIRD

The poor l'ortolan!
One day singing,
then blinded by a chef,
force fed
until three times its size
and drowned alive.
Soaked in brandy
so the humans around me
can savour their gifts
of life and death.

RADIATION

We arrived in Fukushima not long after the disaster
Stepping out from the bullet train into Koriyama City
Sunshine seemed the same, but the air breathed differently
Like it would kill us if breathed too deeply

Something sinister surrounded us, unseen, unfelt or untouched
But we knew it had found us
We knew it could kill us
Not today, not soon
But one day
Too soon
Dust

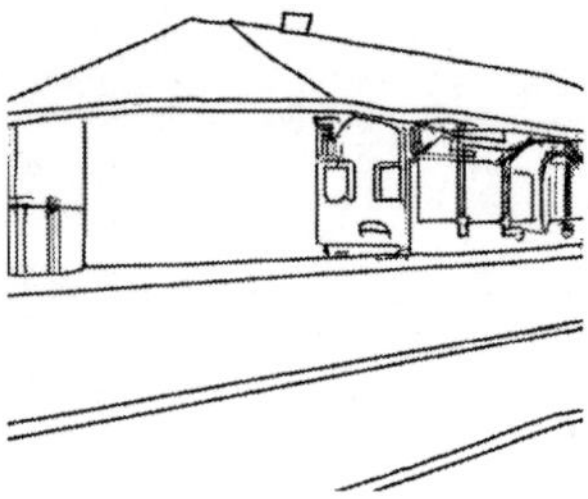

THE TRAIN

As a last resort, there is a railway station where a train leaves at 21:30 and arrives in the direction we need. I agree.

On 03 March 22 we decided that part of our family had to leave Ukraine.

At 17:00 we were in tears and sobs saying goodbye to our daddy. A bridge over the NistruRiver and the unknown awaited us.

17:20 and we are in Moldova. Our passports are stamped and we walk towards the green tent, not knowing what comes next. Outside, it's starting to get dark and it's raining lightly.

A pleasant woman in uniform comes out of the tent and hugs Masha and surrounds us with care.

She leads us to a nearby building where we are fed, watered and warmed. From which my post-vaccination it seems to go over 38. I drink some Nemisil and go to find out how and when we can get to Chisinau.

Volunteers offer to take us to another town, Otaki, where the refugee centre is bigger and there might be another group of people willing to go to Chisinau.

As a last resort, there is a railway station where a train leaves at 21:30 and arrives in the direction we need. I agree.

At 18:30 we find a driver who is willing to take us to a neighbouring village. It is dark outside.

— **Svetlana Gromova**

LONDON

Our two Londons may *be* the same
But *my* London beats yours in every way.
My London inspires me, bribes me
Makes me alive, see.
But your London view
Is only for you.

PADDINGTON

Writers — get up!
Throw up tags and pieces!
Toys and Kings!

SO(M)BRE

The cafe society of England is a picture of sobriety
I wonder what Orwell or Hemmingway would think
of this young fellow who has begun to sink, eaten by his Puffa,
wrapped in grimy off white jeans and grimier white trimmed Vans,
meditating on an empty coffee cup with hidden hands.

IRAN

The random man from Iran
turned up randomly
to our random garden party,
a wild one, particularly strange.
Random Iran man had had no plan,
he'd put a pin in a map, randomly, while his girl was out of town.
Letting fate guide his adventure-day, he'd found his random way to our curious place of Bramshill.
And what a random adventure he had!
Finding us, citizens of four random nations, faking Oktoberfest in a September garden
swilling spirits and beer, dressed as dirndl and Biggles for shits and giggles.
Random Iran left a happy, if confused, man.

FIRST

That familiar first of the year feeling
That one of hope, promise, same old, fear
But not now, not here.
For now I breathe in the air outside
And look with my own eyes
Without stepping inside my own mind
Because in there I'll find
Who knows what calamities this time
And for now, I'm alive

HASHI

Yes. I answered.
"Wow! You can use chopsticks!"
Again. Yes. YES!

GATEBALL

Funehiki, or thereabouts
I went for a wander.

Impassable bamboo forests
Snake nests
Rice fields
Tiny speeding trucks
Suspicious neighbours
Who is this white man?
Vending machines
Sister's business
Special Hair Make Salon
Suddenly, a hall
Inside - ancient townsfolk
Hard worked
Lined and wrinkled
Bent and broken
Headscarf towels
Toothless grins
Playing –

Croquet

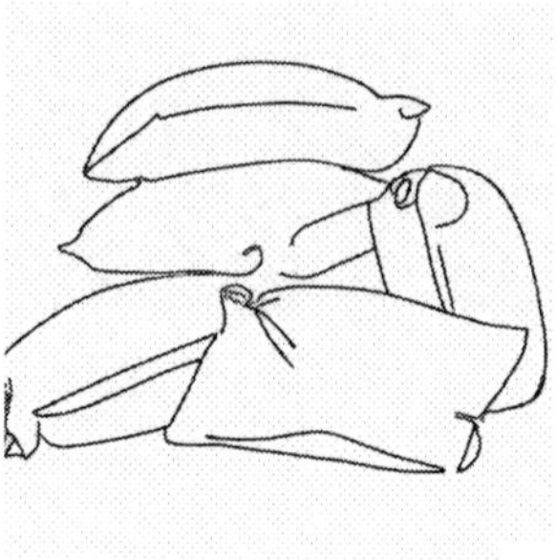

THE HOUSE

Masha starts crying because she is worried how her father will be without us. We get in the car and drive, me, the children, and a man I don't know.

Masha starts crying because she is worried how her father will be without us. We get in the car and drive, me, the children, and a man I don't know. Unfortunately, I didn't get his name. He offered not to drive to Chisinau that night, but to take us to a volunteer centre in Edinet, where we could stay overnight and, in the morning, we could go with renewed energy. And so we did.

The unknown person turned out to be an excellent conversationalist and my brain strain, along with the fever, began to recede.

At 19:40 we arrived in Edinet. Where we were persistently offered another meal. This evening we were the only refugees, and all attention was on us.

At 20:10 we found a place to stay for the night. The volunteer girls offer to bring a duvet and something to wear. Since I don't know where we're going to be taken to a flat, house or gym, I agree to the plaid. We ended up walking out of the centre with a full bag of food, a big warm blanket, a plaid, and some personal hygiene items. The children had backpacks on their shoulders. I was also given a local SIM card. I'm very grateful to this centre and to every volunteer.

Next, we drove with Adrian. A mega-pleasant and kind young man. He helped me to activate my SIM card and gave me 200 lei (£36) for the road to Chisinau.

Adrian drove us to Cosăuti village, where he handed over to Alena and Ivan at a gas station.

At 21:40 we are in a beautiful house. We take a shower, chat, and go to bed.

After all, tomorrow at 05:15 we must get up.

At 05:15 Alena woke us up. We hurriedly got ready and went to the bus terminus in the neighbouring village.

At 05:50 I sat in the half empty bus with the children, and we went in the dark.

It was gradually dawning... I wanted to look at the scenery outside the window, but my eyelids began to slowly fall to my cheeks.

The bus stopped and the driver called me outside... I tensed up... but as it turned out for nothing. He just bought us three teas and a packet of croissants.

Alyona had given me 200 lei for the ride, but the driver refused to take the money for the fare.

At 10:40 we started to meet our distant relative Aunt Raya, as before these events we didn't know each other existed.

Here's the deal.

— **Svetlana Gromova**

VEGAS

3 pm.
I decided to nap.
Tomorrow, New York.
Tonight, mine.
Flight at half seven.
Plenty of time.
Next I knew –
Clock said six.
No! I slept right through.
Quickly quick!
Dammit! I need to pay!
Get me out of here!
Taxi! Go that way!
Like in the movies.
Made it rain.
Ran to desk.
Boom! I'm made!

Huge brown man looked unimpressed.

"Where
are
you
going
tonight,
Sir?"

HIKE

The man and his girl suggested we hike
Come with! It's a nice day!
Just a hike!

We donned flip flops and shorts
Sunglasses. A snack.
Just a hike.

This was Boulder so we biked
to the pickup, ready for this.
Just a hike.

14,000 feet.
Tundra. Burned skin.
Just a hike.

That night we cried.
This was —
Just a Colorado hike.

THRIVE

New start, new shore, new sky
New sight, new sound, new mind.
I chose what came, what stayed behind.
I chose. I changed. I'll thrive.

SLIDES

Are we humans being?
Is being – human?
From spring's cardboard slides
To winter's final silent ride
Our journey passes in blink of eye
Shall we stop and live a while?

PARK

The universal sign for "we will tow your car away if you park it here"
Displayed throughout Milano, big and blue and clear
Is a special sign that to an Italian, says "Park here!"

HARD

"Do you drink hard?" he asked.
The big brown hand
Passed me a big brown rum
For better or worse
Richer or poorer
There was another marriage that day

SUN

Low winter sun
blinds eyes through moving windows.
Again we travel

THE PILOT

During another bombardment they ran to the cellar, the husband was late for a cigarette, and his wife turned around to hurry him up and saw her love torn in two by a Grad shell.

The first few days I grabbed my backpack, the carrier with the two cats and ran to the basement of our 9-story brick building. For three days, maybe. But the explosions were getting closer and more frequent, and with them the understanding became clearer that this basement was not a shelter but a trap: there was only one way out, and when it collapsed no one would be able to get out - the second exit was padlocked and the windows were covered with bricks. So I stopped running to the basement. I lay down on the floor of my tiny bathroom. Not much protection, either, but better than a bed against a window, I thought.

I had no appetite at all, I ate because I had to, cramming a cake, an egg and an apple in my stomach. But I drank a lot of water - I was thirsty all the time. Toilet paper ran out first.

From the first days my older friend Vera called me to her house - they lived on the ground floor, next to the basement, but I was uncomfortable: I had cats, and Vera's place was always clean, and there was family there, and here, again, it was me. And with cats. And their fur and peculiarities of behaviour. But one day, during another bombardment, I realised that if I survived here, I would go crazy with fear. I pushed the struggling cats in the carrier, grabbed my rucksack and called Vera on the run: we are running to you. She said that circumstances have changed, I will not be the only guest, but nothing, will accommodate all, just will not be roomy, and that awaits us.

Her guests were two girls in addition to us, one with a daughter about seven years old and the other eight months pregnant. They were all very quiet, hardly ever leaving the room. The girl only said they couldn't catch their cat when they left, so it stayed at home. They were different, then I understood why: Vera's eldest son, Alexei, drove them out from under fire, literally.

The pregnant girl was the wife of one of his closest friends with whom he had been together since childhood. Alexei bought a house in a village near Chernigov precisely because these guys already lived there. The husband built and fitted out a house for his family himself. The baby the wife was carrying was very long overdue. The husband wanted a girl, Mariyka. There was a front line through the village, it was hell there. During another bombardment they ran to the cellar, the husband was late for a cigarette, and his wife turned around to hurry him up and saw her love torn in two by a Grad shell.

The next day Alexei drove, again under shelling, to collect his friend on a blanket and take him to the morgue - the special brigade refused to go to the area of active hostilities, but he could not leave his friend lying there either.

There were constant air raids, sometimes ten times a day. We were running to the basement. It was very cold, and it was very drafty in there - one of the windows had been broken.

After Alexei had driven the girls away, one day Vera went to the blood transfusion station to donate blood. The station wasn't far, two blocks by the courtyard.

There were air raids all the time. And in one of them, air bombs had been dropped on two neighbouring houses. Vera had to walk past those houses and there was no communication with her. A few hours later she came home, horrified by what she had seen on the way. You may have seen these houses. The whole world has seen them. The pilot who did this was then shot down, he survived and was captured.

As of today, he is not in Ukraine, most probably he was exchanged. Krasnoyartsev is his last name.

When I heard the sound of the fighter jet flying low, I only had time to shout to Vera's husband to move away from the window. The blast wave was thick, palpable.

We were saved by the fact that the flat was downstairs: the glass from upstairs flew out. It only concaves inside the window, it was cold at once.

But the main thing was that we were obscured by another house, where the windows were broken on the opposite side from the calls. I can still see its wall and balcony frames, hanging on one fixture.

47 people died then.

When it became known that several DRGs of Russians had broken into the city and there was a very high chance of street fighting we stopped going to the basement altogether, we lay down on the floor in the corridor. And there were glass doors all around. Each time I wrapped the carrier in a blanket, hoping it would hold back the splinters if they hit it.

On one night when the alarm lasted a few hours I heard an explosion again and through the inner door I saw the glow of fire - a bomb had been dropped somewhere nearby again, so I woke the others to be ready to run if anything happened. Turns out we've learned to black out during an alarm, too.

In all the time I'd been at Vera's - about 10 or 12 days - I'd only run home twice, even though we lived a block away from each other. It was terrifying to go outside. The sky was scary, the walls of houses were scary, every sound was scary. The howl of the air-raid siren could be heard in every sound. Even in the silence. We were constantly questioning each other: was it howling or glitches? Any harsh sound made us jump. But the cats needed litter box litter, we needed food, and there was pasta and tinned food at home, and I was running. There were queues outside at the grocery store. There was an air raid, the city was being bombed and shelled - and people were standing. To buy at least something to eat. Often the electricity and water were cut off - because of the neighbouring houses. But our communal workers were heroes on a par with the AFU and our doctors: they somehow patched up the houses with water, electricity, and gas. They were able to do it at that time.

The city was almost under siege, and it was getting worse every day. Only the bridge over Desna River towards Kyiv was free. Relatively free because the Russians were already standing on the other side and shelling both the bridge and civilian cars. In the village of Yagodnoye, people were already sitting cramped, stuffy, and hungry in the basement of the school, where they had been driven. We learned about this only after the liberation of Yagodnoye.

Every day the authorities said that it was dangerous to leave, that the roads were mined, that the Russians were shelling the roads they had not yet taken, that the Russians refused to cease fire to evacuate the civilians.

– **Tereshenko Svitlana**

NAUGHTY

Have your tickets ready
Stand on the left
Do not obstruct doors
Mind the gap
Give up this seat
Read this
Read that
Penalty if
Feet off seats
Stand behind this
Do not smoke
Offences if
CCTV

Are we all — quite so naughty?

SWIM

One day they paddle
Squealing; delight, dakko
Then they jump
Over tiny waves
Now you watch as
The current bonks
Their little butts
Until one day
They swim away
Further than you,
Way past us

MOVE

Just move down
the fucking train carriage, morons
you won't die

TICKETS

The college kid buries her brows
ready for Mr Tickets
TICKETS please.
Um, my mom said she'd pay and didn't.

OH PLEASE. I need a ticket here.
College kid stalls
But... she said she would and didn't
WHERE are you going?

YOU MUST buy a ticket.
THREE pounds seventy five.
College kid fake winces
Taps her card filled by mom

Mr Tickets winds up to lecture
THIS time I let you go
AND next time you must show –
But college kid has gone

THE GRATITUDE

My children, it's been a year since they saw their daddy.... I hope, I really hope, I pray every night for the war that Russia started to end.

The administrator of the house, Dmitriy, said of course come. On 09 April 22 we moved in. We were very well met and accommodated in a large house by wonderful hosts and their friends. We were helped with food and hygiene. We did not buy anything. All of us were served by different volunteer organisations.

Today is the 14 January 2023. We are still living in this cosy house. In this great time, all the people have become close. There is a good attitude towards each other. We have celebrated all the birthdays here.

My children, it's been a year since they saw their daddy.... I hope, I really hope, I pray every night for the war that Russia started to end.

We all want to go home so badly...

Thank you, thank you so much!!!! To all of Moldova, for such a warm welcome, for such kindness, care and responsiveness.

A big thank you to everyone.

— **Gubanova Julia**

END

If you see
end of line sleepy heads
wake them up

AFTERWORD

Worldwide we approach a hundred million forcibly displaced people as a result of persecution, conflict, violence, human rights violations or events seriously disturbing public order.

1 in 88 people. 20% children.

It's impossible for us to understand the magnitude of the problem and how far it spreads past the current "fashionable" victims.

Hope4 and organisations like them work tirelessly to give some relief, hope, to these people. In buying this book you've helped to feed someone for another week, prevent them from freezing to death, given them a suitcase to replace their plastic bags.

For that I am eternally humbled and grateful.

Find out more about the work of Hope4 at the link below, and if you're so inclined, perhaps donate them a coffee:

https://hope4.org/

ACKNOWLEDGMENTS

Thank you to Chris & Zoe Lomas and all the team at Hope4 for everything you do in the world (except for the weird sea-sick inducing way you used to rock back and forth on video). And thank you to ALL the people fighting the same fight, whether alone as an individual or in one of the many organisations.

Thank you to the contributors who added their voices to give contrast to my words - Alexandra Ievleva, Tereshenko Svitlana, Tatiana Odessa, Svetlana Gromova, Gubanova Julia, and to Ivan Ivancev who translated them.

Thank you to Charli Hunt for editing where I *obviously* thought no edits existed. And re-editing after I rewrote whole sections. Again.

Thank you to DALL-E for the scrappy line drawings, and thank you to Sienna Wright for the amazing cover art. Thank you to Lilia Wright for inspiration to get my thumb out.

And thank you to all the amigos on my LinkedIn who've supported this book through spreading the word, sponsoring pages and generally being very, very lovely humans.

And finally - thanks to you for reading this far.

AWESOME SPONSORS

Everyone on the pages that follow stepped up and sponsored one of the poems in this collection. Mostly, they had no idea what they were about to put their name to so just took a leap of faith in the work that Hope4 are doing so brilliantly. On behalf of everyone that money has helped, may I express my thanks.

Caroline Betz - Glücklich - Happiness (+Marketing) is an inside job. Need help finding joy selling? Join thefcketbucket.com

Lilia Wright - Musky - I want Mars too!

Sienna Wright - Victoria

Placi Espejo - Fuji - "Your mind can seem sometimes like the hardest mountain to climb but once you have got to the top you can truly appreciate the stunning views"

Mandy Fields - Dreamers

Shin-Fei Chen - Tea - "You can never go wrong by being kind." - Shari Carlson

Hilary Mines - Insomnia - The idea is not to live forever, but to create something that does...

Stephen Slater - Services - To request line art drawings of your favourite people, visit www.wearthe.uk or www.linkedin.com/company/weartheuk

Mandy Ward - Home - Everyone has a book in them, with stories to tell, even if it's only your chidren and grandchildren who might ever want to read it. When are you going to write yours?

Elle Moss - Bitter - Together we are stronger https://www.linkedin.com/in/ellemoss/

Jamie Graham - Riverfolk - Copywriting with a magic megaphone - https://wearethehiddenvoices.com/

Martin Zeman - Start - Are you an entrepreneur looking for your Business Leaders' Family? Here it is. https://businessleadersfamily.com/

Matt Phillips - Disturbance - Causing a disturbance in your market, and wondering if PR can help you grow faster? Maybe I can help... mattphillipspr.com.

Tom Bartleet - Electric

Mark Cuthbert - Layby - Taking Occam's razor to data for commercial water conservation www.WhiffAway.com

Erika Borlase - Trained - Journeys and destinations. Make yours to swissfarmhenley.co.uk

Kristen Weatherby - Boracay - The adventure is worth it - resilience helps.

https://www.breakthroughlabs.net/

Yennis Cheung - Kowloon

Manoj Sangany - Gap - "Mindfulness is being mindful of the moment the mind becomes full" https://www.facebook.com/Mindfulmensclub/

Odessa Sherreard - United - Scrivo - I write. We're gifted with words that, when used wisely, can build communities, support those in desperation and stand united in print and page, hearts and minds.

Bhavna Raithatha - Livingstones - Is anyone's life better because you passed their way? https://www.linkedin.com/in/bhavna-raithatha/

Joanne Yulan Jong - NYC - Are you a purpose-driven SME business or brand that needs help with your Sustainability Strategy? We can help. https://yulanc

Sila Nur Isik - Horizon - Follow me, I know the way.

Sarah Clay - Packed - Am I supposed to promote myself here or just write something nice? Hmmm, I'll got with the latter. Cake

Christine Rothman - Flow

Gwilym Davies - Taxi - ...for Gwil. Follow Christopher Wright, he is more clevvvvveeeerrrrrr, better looking and side splittingly funny than I.

Sara Kay - Break - When it's hard to laugh, it's time to laugh hard to de-stress https://www.seriouslaughter.co.uk

Germaine Thurgood - SE19 - Stop the scroll with professional photos!! A fun and creative photographer based in SE19. https://www.germainethurgood.com

Damian Law - A50 - May the sunlight run with you through the forest and light up your way.

David Dyer - Amsterdam - Amsterdam, oh Amsterdam, you led me to Hilversum, and to the love of my life, my wife, thanks Amsterdam!

Karen Wells - GPS - For my dad (1933 - 2021) who taught me values of passion and commitment, kindness and respect. May his legacy continue.

Claire Morley - Seated - "Nothing beats kindness. It sits quietly beyond all things" (Credit: Charlie Mackesy)

David Morley - Hinckley - Just had to follow Claire

Katie Flamman - Glass - Doesnt your story deserve a decent voiceover? www.storyteller-media.com

Lucien Wynn - Redeye

Annabelle Filer - Arrival - Changing poverty through The Second Harvest. Old wisdom, new beginnings. tensei.co.uk

Neal Veglio - Hole - I sound like the radio & I'm really rather cross about podcasting done badly. And I used to be famous

Jill Hood - Meet

Dave Officer - Scone - I'm just here for a story about scones.

Michiel Den Haerynck - Left - Always right.

Vanessa Ashworth - Carry - Exasperation requited, Branding righted, Visibility highlighted. Prospects incited, To Bite! - Strategic B2B Marketing

Andy David - Side-eye - Be excellent to each other.

Frew Murdoch - Boatman

Charli Hunt - Picadilly - 100 sponsors? It's like Piccadilly Circus in here.

Christine Armstrong - Winchester - Wrightee's favourite vlogger from Winch. Possibly.

Zoe Denning - Coin - Master your business finances through the power of Xero cloud accounting software https://xeroforsmes.co.uk/

Ges Ray - Lawn - He sang of Triumph! Such a man knoweth his Speak Performance skills: https://speakperformance.online

Radek Stejskal - Land - Everybody can contribute to a better, kinder and more compassionate world.

Jason Bissell - Steps - One Step, keep stepping... thenhow.com

Ana-Maria Ignat-Berget - Daughters - When things get hard dont disappear through the webs of distractions. Lets daydream together to unlock ideas for a better future. ideasunlocked.com

Lorraine Venables - Bird - When you learn, teach. When you get, give.

Maya Angelou, I Know Why the Caged Bird Sings

https://www.linkedin.com/company/intrepid-english/

Basil - London - You can take the dog out of the city. But you can't take the city out of the dog.

Proof Content - Thrive - Cheers to the best Key Messaging Strategist (and SaaS start-up owner, website architect, video guy, LinkedIn vlogger and now poet) there is!

Amy Stokes-Waters - Sun - Already got a daughter, and now I have a sun.

Gillian Cobb - Naughty - "Sometimes you have to be a little bit naughty" from Matilda, the musical

Andy David - Move - And party on, dudes!

Timea Kadar - Tickets - The right people. The right place. 50+ networking events a year in Private Members Clubs in London.

https://franciscooper.com/lbs/

Steve Wright - End - The distance may be far but it's words that brings us together.